SOUL

SISTERS

Parted by Land Not by Soul

Madhurima Modak & Chanda Jaiswar

This book is dedicated to our higher self.

It's a dedication to my eternal love Sumedh.

~ Madhurima

Preface

What is this book about? What do we actually wanna say through these Pages ? How is "SOUL SISTER" benefiting you?

If we have to say, so we can say Soul Sister is about two late-teenager's journey from troubling to learning, from confusion to clarity, from human body to soul, from lust to tantra, from nothing to everything, from money to universal abundance, from non awakened to enlightenment, from long distance online friends to SOUL SISTERS.

It's a testimony of becoming LOVE. Finding your own way to meet yourself. Leading your reality, living best life that exists in this vast multiverse.

How mobile phones and social media, if used correctly can become your way to your higher self too. We used this medium to not only get connected with each other but also we write this entire book over the phone.

Our first blockbuster series, a psychological thriller named "AADAT" is releasing soon on OTT platform.

Thank you so much for all your support.

Content

"'Cause you are that someone
That gets me like no one else
Right when I need it the most
And I'll be the one you rely on
A shoulder to cry on
A friend through the highs and the lows"

~ (Alone pt. 2 by Ava max, Alan Walker)

These lines are expressing exactly that we really feel for each other.

Let's start the Journey...

NOT AWAKENED

WHERE EVERYTHING STARTED

"The sky has to be dark enough for the stars to shine"

~ Madhurima

This chapter is the first initial days of our journey to ourselves. It's telling you all about the first stage of our story in the journey of us meeting our souls within. WHERE EVERYTHING STARTED is nothing but the dusk phase after a sunset, the time when the sky started getting darker for the stars to show up.

When you destined to do something and didn't even know what it is, but surely knowing there's something. you are in search but not knowing exactly for what your soul is seeking. But when it meant for you, it always ended up happening, no matter what. Somewhere deep inside your soul knows everything. When you started walking to meet your soul, in order to explore yourself, your higher self that exists vastly in the multiverse. In between this self actualization journey life happens, until you realize the game and take the control. Some people get stuck but some dare to dive into this journey of being one with their higher version or best version.

It's 2018. Two 16 years old teen girls were troubling with nothing but their own selves. But as mentioned before if it is destined, you're gonna realize everything as Chanda and Madhu did. Their story began with LOVE, for LOVE. A journey not only to meet their own soul and purpose but also to end the search , to find the Soul connection of eternity , to be together with their soul tribe again, to be Soul sisters again, that they used to be before their incarnation in this 3d world.

And here you go...

CHANDA'S POV

Okayyy !!! So When Everything Started ??

The situation began when I felt disconnected from those around me. I realized that some relationships were not as genuine as I had believed. While I value the people in my life, I sometimes seek validation from others. Despite caring for those around me, I often felt that I didn't receive the same level of attention and consideration in return, which impacted my self-esteem.

During this period, I found inspiration in a celebrity, whom I initially considered my first Crush . I first saw him on television and felt a strong connection. Intrigued, I searched for him on Instagram and found that he had achieved a childhood dream of becoming an actor. His story motivated me, reinforcing the belief that dreams can come true with self-confidence.

{ we all went through a "love crisis" situation at some point of our lives. But the problem that they do figure out is, it's nothing but lack of self love. The hunger for love could be filled with only by filling you self love cup. It might sound a lil bit annoying if you're in a situation where your need of love on its peek. So please trust me, on this one. Once you start loving yourself, you prioritize yourself and your self worth get increased. So what happens is you started to radiate LOVE. And guess what ? Everyone around you, love you as much as you love yourself. Because simply this reality is a mirror of your inner world. But Chanda didn't even realize the importance of self love back then, as no one tells. Sad part in India we have to learn all this on our own or from internet. But it should be told by our parents and teachers. }

I distinctly remember this was during my 12th grade, with board exams approaching in February 2019. I first noticed him in November 2018 . Although his show had premiered in October 2018, I initially hesitated to watch it due to my busy schedule with college.

Initially, I decided not to watch the show but later felt a strong urge to do so. As time passed, my exams went well, and my long vacation began. I started watching his show extensively, along with his previous works. On my 17th birthday, I experienced a personal setback, leading me to reevaluate my friendships and eventually distance myself from certain individuals.

I became deeply engrossed in following him, which helped me temporarily escape from my personal issues and find happiness in my own company. This led me to become more introverted, but I was content with this change as it brought me joy.

One day, I decided to create a fan page for him to stay connected and feel closer to him. Despite having no prior experience managing an Instagram fan page, I took the initiative and started one. Looking back, I sometimes find it hard to believe that I actually created a fan page for him..

I fully support the 17-year-old version of myself who found happiness in admiring him. My feelings for him were strong.

Creating a fan page was like building a virtual world for myself. Initially, only a few people followed my page, and being an introvert, I hadn't followed anyone back. However, the algorithm worked in my favor, and his content frequently appeared in my explore section, bringing me joy.

One day, a girl from the fandom messaged me after seeing my story. She was the first person I interacted with in the fandom, and I was amazed by her ability to engage in a continuous one-hour conversation with a stranger. Her confidence impressed me, especially considering my own discomfort with talking to strangers. She was the second account I followed, marking the beginning of our bond.

I was quite shy during our initial phone calls. I mostly responded with brief phrases like "yes," "okay," and "alright." However, this contrast between her talkative nature and my reserved demeanor has become a unique aspect of our bond, with her being the chatterbox and me, the attentive listener.

Interestingly, we both created our fan pages on the same day, March 27th. Her name is Madhurima, but I affectionately called her "Modhu,".

 I admire her so much that I can openly express my feelings for her and everyone else without fear of judgment.

{ it's a quite nostalgic for us, we're doing our final editing of this book today and while reading this part it just clicked that today the last episode will gonna be telecast.}

On her first birthday after we became friends, I wished her exactly at midnight and even created a post for her,

although I never ended up posting it or telling her about it. I was very conscious about my actions and concerned about what others might think.

A week later, she called me excitedly to inform me about a quiz competition organized by the show's production they posted on their social handle , exclusively for Mumbai residents. The prize was a chance to meet our idol in person and If I win, she'll also be able to talk to him over the phone. I was thrilled and eager to participate.

MADHU'S POV

You already read her part of where everything had begun. So it's all that damn fan page, we had to make. I believe that it's a part of our destiny ahead, what we have been building since then. So mine is a little different but not so much, because y'all should know that me and her belong to the same soul tribe.

It's 2018 then, I was in 12th. A random evening it was, mumma was watching a mythological daily soap tv show and I saw him for the very first time on TV. Who knows that he is gonna be my forever, my twinflame. I don't know why from that very moment that one person started living in my heart and mind rent free. Maybe I had watched him before in promos or any reality show but I can't remember vividly because I never noticed him nicely, but that day was different when I saw him. So normally like any other person, I rushed to Google him by his character he was playing, that I didn't even know his name though. For my 12th boards I had my phone but no access to the internet, typical Indian family you know. But I'm a stubborn type of a person, and now it comes to Love, ahhhhh my soft spot. So mumma's mobile hotspot made this happen for me. With an excuse of checking study materials I had started to explore that guy, for a few days. Then I stopped because I had to focus on my boards. But secretly I kept checking on this guy always, i can't help it.

It was March 13th, 2019 my boards were over. I was like "Ab toh time hi time hai pyaar mein doob jaane ke liye". To be very honest I didn't even know how to use Instagram properly, LMAO. So I just changed my existing account name to make a fan page and as y'all know fandom means creativity (arts, edits, videos etc.). I just started to sketch and I became very good at it just by love. I'm a person who only drew the body anatomy in biology class. So this is how the fan page was created on 27th March,2019.

Coincidentally she had created her fan page on that same day. And Boom ! The door had opened, the door of our destiny, of love, of growth. Initially a destiny path had led us then we started choosing our own one among all destiny paths.

We had started talking in comments and DM, I just died laughing while writing this, like formalities and fake compliments. Due to lower self concept often we made fun of our own selves by not accepting that we are good enough. There's so much difference between now and those initial days. I do remember when I first talked with this girl (maybe it was the first week of April), so shy, so quiet, introverted. And me ? Like always loud, 'jhinga lala hoo hoo' type of person. To be very honest we two are entirely opposite by nature. But gradually we started talking more often, most of the time the topic was fanpage and idol.

I still remember it's just one month to our friendship but I was way too much concerned about her. As she said she wanted to be an actress, so yeah she used to go for random auditions. One day she was a lil late and I got too worried because she didn't pick up my calls, the rest she realized when she had heard my trembling voice.

I actually didn't know what the connection between us was, I always felt like there was something special about this girl. Her real name is Chanda but she's Sapna to me for her fanpage. I don't know why but I cared about her so much, it feels like I knew her for so long.

Don't worry readers we're gonna explore together "What's our bond !? Why is she and me destined to be together..."

But you know what nothing is co-incident, everything is happening for something there's always a bigger picture we couldn't get to see, which we'll realize by time.

Yeah Yeah you all got it right. These two has same idol, but the magic is that complicates nothing. Everything happens for the best, for real. Every story has its own twists and turns.

WINNING THE CONTEST

"Sometimes we win, sometimes we loose ,

in between loosing & winning , we rise as new person"

~ Chanda

Winning the contest ~ We won the competition, loses our friendship , and rise as bestie.

So the title already said it all, yes this chapter is all about WINNING a contest. But had they really won ? If every win brings joy, why did this one bring sorrow? This question always remained. As previously mentioned, it was a contest held by that TV Show production where our idol was a lead actor that time. So yeah that time both of us thought that it was a golden opportunity for both of us to meet him. But the contest was for only Mumbai residents, so Chanda got the opportunity not Madhu. But Madhu was equally excited.

Contest rules were the easiest we just had to answer three questions related to the show.

But the thing is whoever answers first, got more chances to win. So Madhu always answered first for Chanda, if she's not online. And guess what, She won. One week later a DM had come from the production about the details and all.

MADHU'S POV

We both are so powerful when it comes to manifesting since then. We actually manifested that "Win", both of our energies worked together to win this contest. But the thing is back then we were not aware of our powers and manifestations. Now it's just waiting for a few days till 20th May, (2019) and prepping some gifts for our idol.

CHANDA'S POV

What gift should I give him? I struggle with choosing gifts for people. Thankfully, I have Madhu , she helped me in choosing gift.

The night before our meeting was incredibly special. I felt a mix of excitement, nervousness, and happiness, making it feel like the longest night ever. Finally, I was going to meet our idol in person. Morning arrived quickly, and time seemed to fly by. I didn't want to be late. Transportation had been arranged by the production team.

*_MADHU'S POV_*

I can remember so vividly my excitement about that day. Not only her, I was going with her too but virtually. And why shouldn't I get excited!! As we did everything together from answering the Contest questions to gift preparation. So yeah she made a promise there, that she was going to show HIM my arts and if possible she was going to make a phone call so that I can talk to HIM even if it's a 2 min call. But when she reached there, her network had started to disturb. The data wasn't working 0.1%. As we knew about the network disturbance there, i never mind that. She was totally disconnected, just texted me a few about the update. And I was just waiting and waiting and waiting since afternoon, to talk with him. It feels so silly now when I'm writing it all down but yeah that time we all were less matured, and I just thought back then it's my first and last chance to talk with him, the him I loved the most.

It's 11 pm, she didn't even text me a single thing. And I got an update that she was in the car, way back to home. I was so clueless at that time, I didn't even know what happened. That night went.

Next day I knew that she had to go to her native house which is in Varanasi. That day I cried, I cried like there was no tomorrow. Mumma caught me crying and asked, I lied to her that I was just nervous for my 12th results. I just couldn't describe the feeling to anyone, because I don't even know what to say. Our friendship got questioned if I said anything, which I never wanted to happen. Because I love her man, I fucking love her.

This Billie Eilish song

"And I don't talk shit about you on the internet

Never told anyone anything bad

'Cause that shit's embarrassing, you were my everything

And all that you did was make me fucking sad"

It describes it all.

Time flies, after almost a week we started talking again, I don't know what's my fault but I apologized and tried to make things normal.

CHANDA'S POV

Actually, that location is quite near to Gujarat. It's called Umargam, and everyone was aware of the network issues there. The other winners and I arrived around 2-3 pm, and the shoot was ongoing. We were told to wait in a room, and that wait lasted until night. We finally got to meet him at 10 pm after the shoot wrapped up. Can you imagine?

But that's a fact. After that, they had their own plans for a cake-cutting ceremony to celebrate a milestone achieved by the show. Their schedule was so busy, with numerous interviews that night. During the wait, my phone died, even I couldn't take any selfies with him. I only have a single photo taken on someone else's phone. As a result, I didn't get a chance to call and let her talk to him.

I felt so grief-stricken and embarrassed because of that. When we were returning home at 11 pm, I tried to turn on my phone, and it powered on with just 1%. I texted her, and then my phone died again. The next day, I told her everything that happened and how little time we had to meet him. For that, I was trolled and attacked by fandom members. Everyone posted stories against me because they didn't believe me. That was the worst feeling ever because that incident made me seem selfish.

I called her and explained about the stories, as she was the only person I had told about what happened there. She insisted she hadn't shared anything with anyone. I cried on the phone and then hung up. Even now, my question remains unanswered: "Who told everyone?"

Well Several minor incidents occurred, and we stopped talking. Then I went back to my hometown.

MADHU'S POV

So as we all know that time heals every goddamn thing, even if TIME is a social construct (it's not real tho). Our issues faded away as the wheel of time started to spin. Because whatever happened, it's not our fault. It's just our unconscious fear, that came true. No matter how immature they were that time, the LOVE was the same. Arguments, disagreements, ups and downs come hand in hand with every relation, but we never break the bond for that. They gave each other the time they needed in order to be okay and soothe. Thank God we never ended up breaking our friendship, otherwise who's gonna write this book. Even the thought of "they're getting parted" frightened them enough today. But anyways that's not our destiny, we have to stay together and have to make a lot of things happen together, as we did. That's why we happened to each other. It's exactly what this book is about, our freaking magical story. It's just the beginning, we never thought that we have such miracles in our lives to experience Keep exploring with us, there's so much to learn ahead.

KNOWING US

What I wanted to do in my life,

led to the Question Who am I ?

~ Chanda

REACH OUT.
AMY_MOONS

OPEN UP.

Only 27% of people do jobs based on their academic stream and half of India's teenagers or even adults don't even know what they wanna do in their life. How to generate an income source by following your passion and some crackerjack people don't even know what their passion is, what gives them real happiness, what satisfies their souls. They can actually live their life of dreams by doing something they really love to do. And some people who do know their passion, wrong information by wrong people and internet drives them in a path where they get demotivated. And this has happened to those mostly who choose "Money over Happiness and Peace".

And in between all these doubts and chaos one should prioritise themselves, not any friend's suggestions who is not enough experienced. They just don't even have the knowledge you seek, about what you want to do. You should ask those Friends who tell you at least one positive thing , who believe in you , in your talent, not to those who are always running behind the trending career options. Seriously guys I'm telling you to stay away from those negative people because they have a problem for every solution.

So basically our advice to them who don't know what to do in life, "don't need to panic everyone has their own spark, different style and seriously listen to your own intuition "

Do what you feel is right even if it seems wrong to other people, because at the end of the day you matter and there's nothing wrong. No matter what your neighbour aunty is commenting on, no matter if someone commented about your passion that "it's a waste of time". We need to clear one thing here that by not doing anything, ultimately you're wasting time. So something is much better than nothing.

We must be a curious soul and we believe everyone has that learning capacity & curiosity it's just contrast level are different.

And at the end of the day or week (up to you) we should ask ourselves "What I've learnt new today?" even if it is just a new word. It could be from a movie, an Instagram post or any kind of book. When we were struggling about our stream like Madhu was clear that she's going to take admission in D.ED & complete her graduation first. but as you all know very well only few people makes career on based of their academic. same Madhu was not aware about what's she actually wants to do in her life because she was not happy with her academic choices even though she's scholar and other side Chanda had really clear vision about her career that she wanted to become an actor. She never made Plan B for herself. But because of the parents, it was necessary to complete her graduation at least .She was so messed up about her choices of streams because didn't want to give time in college.

MADHU'S POV

Time was flowing at its own rhythm, and we were trying to catch it up. But how we can merge ourselves with something (time) that doesn't even exist universally. I still don't like time tho. But in this 3d world, we have this mf TIME with us forever. With the flow of time , our 12th board results came out. Now its time for our admissions to the next courses.

"But what should we do after 12th", yes like other students, this question had pushed us to a cyclone of options. I thought at that time, as I wasn't aware of the unlimited potential I do possess and the infinite possibilities I can have. So basically I scored pretty much good like 90% in WBCHSE and especially 95 in "Computer application" so I thought I should do BCA. But then I found out I was under-age , I passed my 12th when i was 17+

So yeah there's two options left for me. One was to wait one year or in the meantime try something else. My papa told me to take admission in D.El.Ed (it's a teacher's training course to be a teacher at the elementary level), so I did. And yeah no matter how much I did curse this course but I'm still grateful for everything that happened afterwards.

So my admissions were done so smoothly but initially I didn't like that place, new people new place that means a new me too. Because I've a chance to express and explore a new me. But to be very honest I didn't like that back then, I was so pissed off and mad at me for taking such a decision. I wasn't so much adaptable to new stuff that time in comparison to current time. But that time I had to continue with that. One good thing among such annoying ones is we didn't have to study hard there, it's a professional course so it's more of a projects and activities based thing. 2019 Madhu had to deal with those new people and circumstances along with something you know right!!! Yes you guessed it right, it's that goddamn fanpage. Most of you know how hectic it is to run a fanpage. For some particular moment mine academic streams was clear but Chandaa ! sometimes I got a headache for her she didn't even know what to do. I guess her reaction was the same for me, because I didn't know what to do in life either !

I still remember Chanda used to explain to me a lot about career options and importance. What to do in life and all even though she was struggling with her own academic choices she always tried to push me to know about the new stuffs , to explore, to step out of the limits. But none of these bothered me that time, and I kept being the same. And if I put this too much honestly I was lost, or more precisely lost in hopeless Love which also sounded like "*pagalpan*". But Chanda kept explaining what's right for me, good for me, but that dumb-head me was so hopelessly romantic, couldn't get what she said at all. Maybe because that's not my time to get this all in. My true self was still sleeping somewhere in me, waiting for me to wake her up and explore.

I was also going through some changes that felt weird so aimlessly lost that time, but it's a phase for everyone like me who doesn't know what to do in life after 12th or even graduation for some of you, which I can understand and know how to deal with now lately.

We were omniscient & free counselors for each other but deep inside we both were messed up actually ! I'm more than her but the undeniable truth is she's the same as me so all went to in vain, "Ax on my own foot" that's what actually happened . So both of us were fucked up. we both got stuck in some kind of turbulence without any direction.

But as a 17 y/o we should have done our Graduation first (typical India parents things) , so now Chanda was in trouble, she's gonna narrate to you the whole way she figured it all out.

CHANDA'S POV

Sometimes, our greatest strength can also be a vulnerability, especially when it comes to family. While they can be our biggest supporters, they may not always understand our choices due to generational differences. Things have changed since the '80s and '90s; it's no longer just about passing 10th or 12th grade for a government job.

Nowadays, we have more career options, educational opportunities, and work possibilities than ever before. Even Gen Z has innovative ideas for both active and passive income. However, families might not always see the value or profit in these new ideas.

When a family does support, the next challenge often becomes financial and time constraints. This can force a person to adapt to their circumstances. My passion for art has been known to everyone around me since childhood, but it's never been taken seriously. I was always told that passing 10th and 12th grade was crucial for my future and societal acceptance. Fearing judgment, I chose to pursue science in 12th grade, even though art is where my true passion lies. I later regretted this decision, feeling like I was wasting my time. While my family didn't pressure me into choosing science, societal expectations and assumptions from everyone around me influenced my decision. Looking back, I wish I had followed my heart and pursued art instead.

Assumption makes reality, make assumptions for yourself as you want otherwise other's assumption will be your reality.

I somehow managed to pass 12th grade, driven by my desire to break free from the traditional education cycle and pursue my dreams. After 12th, I intended to choose an easier subject to have more time for my passion. However, I ended up enrolling in a BSc program instead.

Most of you can relate to whatever was happening in our lives. But you know what everything will always find its own way to work out, even if it feels so damn wrong at that very moment but that always leads you to exactly where you needed to be. Same in Madhu and Chanda's life here, they were just 17 y/o then and all of the situations were fucked up. But they keep going, keep walking into the fog of the future , not knowing what next. But one thing they were definitely doing is "LIVING THE PRESENT". No matter what happened or whatever they were doing aimlessly but they lived their own fucking lives as good as possible. They never even had a thought to give up, kept on going, as we all should.

MADHU'S POV

Already gave you a lot of heavy lectures (Gyan) but you know why I wasn't getting time to think about my own life!!! I know it sounds so cringe but yeah, I was so busy with my fanpage and idol. You know what, I'm a kinda person of Love, "pyaar ke liye jaan kurbaan" types. And I was just 17, late teenage, different level of hormonal changes, you know.

So yeah I'm saying shamelessly that I totally ignored my life and got busy with my fanpage. Like making posts and retagging to get noticed, collaboration, arts, stalk him, blah blah blah!!! Jeezzz !!! Even now when writing it sounds so toxic, actually it is. After all this, next we got jealousy ,back bitching, frustration etc that comes free with the fanpage. Fandoms are so toxic, if you know you know. So for months, a lot of my time was spent in this fandom (maybe its Aug 2019) and then simultaneously the preparation for HIS b'day gifts was going on. That's a whole different story, let's leave some stories for my other books too.

This is how my online life was going on, but my offline life was fucked up. College attendance and activities are okay but here's a fact that the more you come closer to your online buddies, the more your offline friendships fade away. until you're not more than good to manage friendships. But my scenario is kinda different, because of my different course and college, I already got separated from them as my friends were in general Colleges. I was kinda friendless, I was connected to all but on a surface level . Maybe I never had friends really. Old connections were cutting their threads as well as the new ones were connecting, both online and offline. But yes it took me a lil long to get comfortable with all of these changes.

I started getting new experiences in college, if you're someone who has been in these kinda diploma professional courses so you could know that those institutes become like a family. The same happened to me.

The very first day I cried into my pillow because I didn't like that place everyone is unknown and seniors, all of my "so called friends" are together in college and I'm the only one who's there kinda stuff but as time flies it became my fav place. So my offline stuffs were lil bit stable for sometime as of then. That I didn't even realise that Chanda is gonna be the most important part of my life.

Like it is said, you met some people for a reason, I met Chanda because it was written by the stars. She's a blessing to me and always will be.

CHANDA'S POV

Okayy so after taking advice how I ended up taking BSC ??

so the reason is that time it was so easy to influence me , at some point I had no guts to stand for myself in front of family

Madhu kept saying "Chanda tu tere mann ka kar , ye teri choice honi chahiye agar tujhe nahi karna hai science to chhod de "

I didn't want to disappoint my family, especially since my dad was proud of my decision to pursue science. Despite my attempts to communicate my preference for BA over BSc, my dad responded, "If you want to do BA, why not do it from Varanasi instead of Mumbai?" Without further argument, I enrolled in BSc, despite having little interest in science. Some people questioned my choice, not realizing that BSc can be challenging for those not passionate about the subject.

Every day, my friend Madhu and I discussed life, love, and how to navigate challenging situations. We never ran out of topics to talk about. And let's not forget about our fanpage!

Time flew by, and before I knew it, October arrived along with exams. Due to my lack of interest in science, I was unprepared and ended up failing three subjects. I decided not to retake the exams and didn't care about what others had to say. This time, I informed my family and friends about my decision rather than seeking their permission. Fortunately, my dad supported me.

I left my course halfway through the year to focus on acting. I started attending auditions and acting seminars. One incident that brought tears of happiness was when I returned from a seminar with a dead phone battery. Madhu was worried when she couldn't reach me, calling me over 15 times and sending messages to make sure I was okay.

She tried every possible way to contact me, and her efforts meant a lot to me. It was a touching moment that made me emotional. After taking a break, I realized I needed to better prepare myself. While I'm confident in front of a camera and can perform in front of hundreds of people, I struggle with one-on-one conversations and lack communication skills.

I remembered that I knew some people who had a YouTube channel with a decent number of subscribers and produced music.

I told Madhu about this and she was like "itne time tak ruki huyi kyu thi ab jakar khyal aa raha hai" So next day I contacted one of my common friend

Rumi says "what you seek is seeking you"

They were looking for a model for their videos, so we ended up shooting three videos together. The videos were well-received, and despite leaving my studies halfway through the year, I continued learning and didn't waste my time. I added value to my profile .

So this is how their 2019 went. This year was a little bit messy yet so important. As this year a chapter ended and a big one had begun unknowingly. Waves of changes, new beginnings in both professional and personal life. In between this Chaos two late teenagers and "going to be adults" started walking with trembling steps, but they were still walking though without falling out. FALLING is something mandatory when we didn't know the paths clearly. But if we never fall, how do we gonna rise ?

Yeah, they fell badly to raise more stronger to walk more wiser. Their next few months story aka the 2nd phase, we are taking you through the journey of rise and fall.

Choose Your Words Wisely

They say "Words have energy and power with the ability to help, to heal, to hinder, to hurt, to harm, to humiliate and to humble."

Indeed !!

But still weren't consciously aware about our words, what we were saying as joke or in serious conversations. We should be fully aware of words , because subconscious mind doesn't not differentiate between serious talk or joke .It records everything 24/7. Once in a conversation.. Chanda wasn't realise what she said that will be going to cost her 6 months.

Sometimes we bored by staying in same place , we want some changes , what kind of change we want we know already !! If you don't know then you should know about your desire because if you don't clear about your thoughts then you might speak some sentences that you really don't want in actual life .

We say something for someone in anger that actually we didn't want for them. Subconscious mind or you can say Universe doesn't differentiate between good or bad. Because Good & Bad both are equal in some perspective !!

Chanda didn't realise that she said that "I wants to go somewhere out of Mumbai for 6 months , then everyone will going to miss me". She doesn't clear the Place where she actually wanna go or Is it really she wanted to go from Mumbai ??

No !!!

But She said and forget and it came into realisation after a week , when her Dad told her that we're going to Hometown.

After a month he will came back and Chanda going to stay for 6month because of Lockdown there's nothing to do in Mumbai. And There She realised her power of words. She had not any option except to stay there for 6 Months.

That's why "Choose your words wisely" !!

DISORIENTED

(FRIENDS TO STRANGERS)

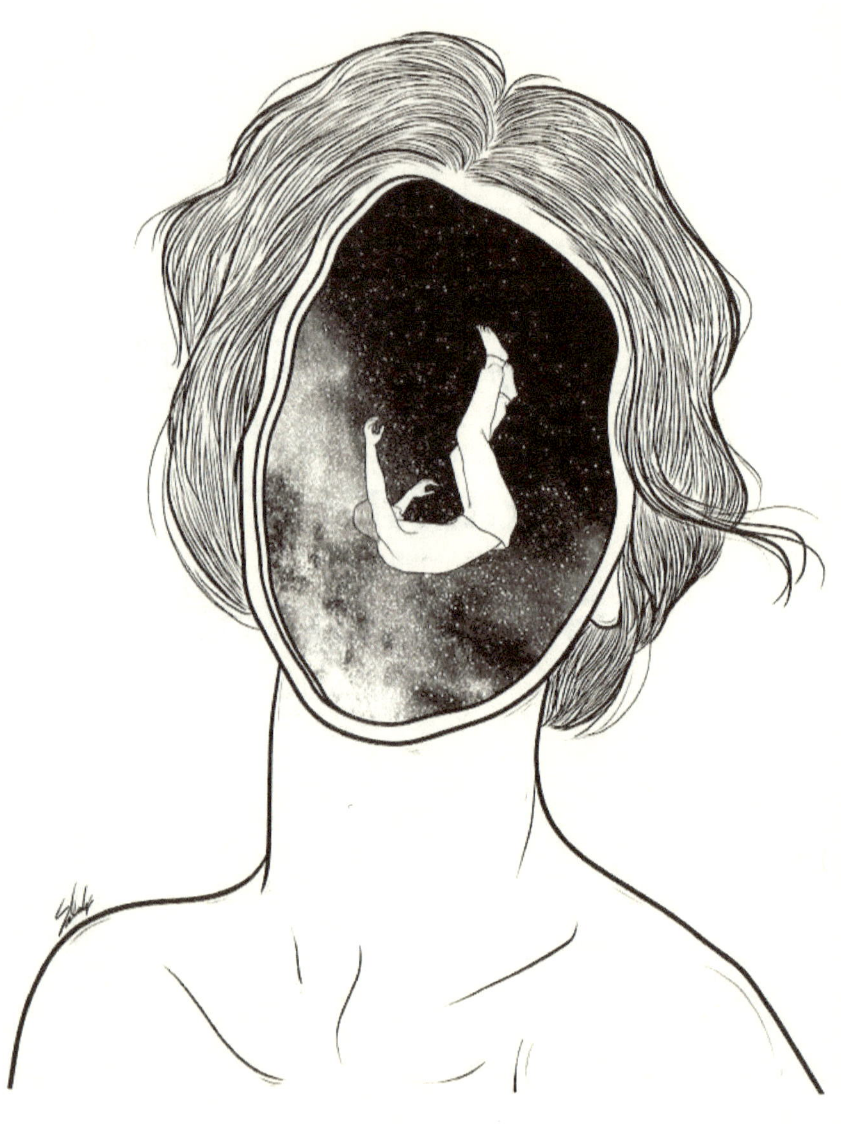

DISCONNECTING

"Nothing can part us, not even Land

It just we...

Universe separated us, to make us realise each other's worth. "

~ Chanda

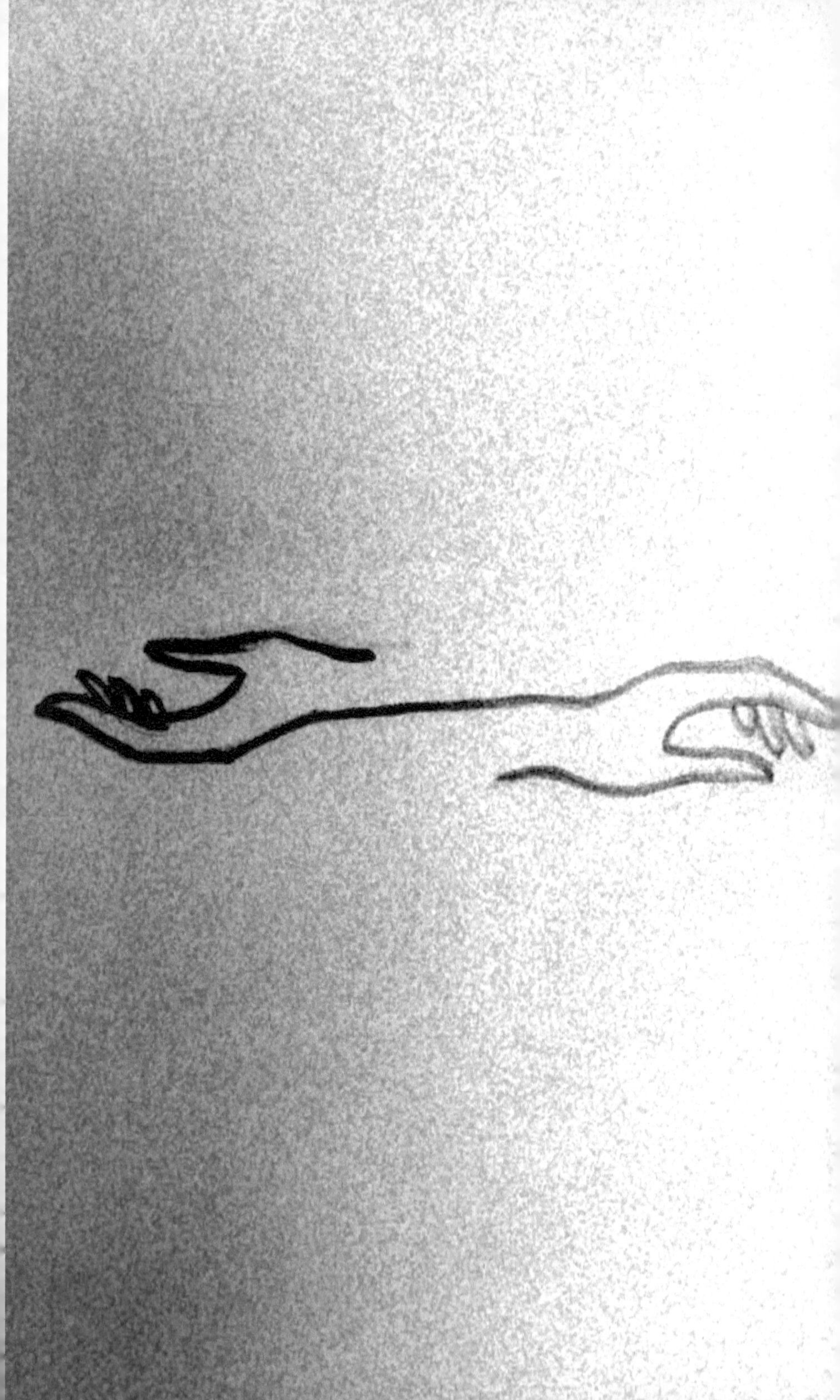

It was already March, 2020 and the news of an unknown virus was trending. But we people of India weren't aware enough of that yet. One day I just came back home from college and suddenly out of nowhere the news headline screamed "The complete Lockdown will be starting on 24th March for one week straight ". Back then we didn't even know what that word 'Lockdown' exactly means in real. Then lockdown extended and extended and extended. The world got locked in home and paralyzed with the fear of a virus named COVID-19. Madhu and Chanda was also going through the same. Initially Madhu, Chanda and lots of people like them was happy because it seemed like a long vacation until they all experienced the fear. The fear of health, losing people, losing life, blurry vision of their future and the list is kept going. This is how March came to us like an absolute disaster.

*_CHANDA'S POV_*

News about Covid-19 was spreading rapidly in India, but it seemed like the news was spreading faster than the virus itself. I remember how confidently my friends and I dismissed the possibility of the virus reaching India. Despite the challenges of 2020, it was a year of learning and gaining life experience. I was fortunate to meet some wonderful people both online and offline. Madhu was always by my side, and I also made new friends who became like a second family to me. It was a new and enriching experience to connect with people without any specific reason, to call each other just to chat, and to learn valuable life lessons from friends. Everything seemed to be going well between my family, friends, and our YouTube videos. Life felt fulfilling, not like a dream, but a happy reality. As March approached, my birthday month, Madhu surprised me with a special gift.

(guys you can imagine crying emoji here)

The gesture left me thinking, "Does someone really do this much for someone else?" We hadn't even met in person yet, and she went out of her way to make me feel special. She had sent me a handmade card, a sketch of me, earrings, a handmade bookmark, and some thoughtful notes. When I called her, I was on the verge of tears because it was the first time someone had made such an effort to make me happy. However, as time went on, I'm not sure what happened between us; we became increasingly distant. I was unaware when Madhu had an accident involving a bus. Letting bygones be bygones.

A long journey always requires time. It felt as though I was on a never-ending bridge or highway, unsure of Madhu's whereabouts. Was she left behind or waiting for me at the highway's end? Now, I understand that this journey was crucial, as it allowed me to discover profound insights and emotions about life.

MADHU'S POV

"It takes two to Tango."

We need both of our hands to clap, as in any relationship both are responsible for anything. So the disconnection was not only felt from Chanda but also there was equal reciprocation of mine. Chanda and me both didn't know that much in detail what was going on in each other's lives.

Meanwhile that COVID-19 and Lockdown flipped our lives upside down, it's quite natural because new normals were messed up.

Life had taken a long pause in Lockdown, all we had, was our mobile phone and social media. The free time was making our phone even more boring. Online classes are frustrating. If we sit and think about that time, already it makes me feel useless. We all became BUNNY (passive version) from *"Yeh Jawani hai Diwani ke Bunny"* and we were observing *"Waqt ko guzarte"*. So now you all may know what I was supposed to do that time, yeah attending online classes and running my fanpage. The amount of blunders and mistakes I made there, became a lesson to me. But now it all sounds funny. Fandom is a place where most of the people are lowest valued and self esteemed, toxic to be very honest. They breathe jealousy. Now you might think how much jealousy a person could possibly have?! I don't know to what extent you can think but I got trapped in jealousy and negative people (even they falsely accused me for cyber bullying). It's personal advice (especially to my teen readers) if you are in a fandom, just stay neutral, if you're not mentally prepared and matured. And if you're strong enough it's all up to you.

So basically I decided to give up on life because of course lack of maturity and mental strength. That incident felt like a curse, I was so ashamed of myself, not my fault at all but I suspected me. It was like hell, got stressed, got hair falls and that stress gifted me PCOD/PCOS.

But somehow it was passed and one of the biggest lessons it gave me was to "control my anger issues". A small initial but crucial step towards my growth.

This incident turned out as a turning point of my life, it had actually pushed me to the edge. There's a saying that "everything is a blessing in disguise". This incident was that and so the lockdown was.

 So I had two options, one was to take a step forward even though everything seemed foggy or otherwise I had fallen in the worst case scenario. However I gathered the courage to take a step and live my life in the best ways possible. And that's exactly when my actual journey started.

The path of Friends to Strangers was easy that time. Because this phase had started before their friendship touched one year mark. So we can say "The thread started to get loose, yet it was just slightly tight.

And in 2020 l, that thread got completely torn except one single string, universe knows which unknown invisible 'string' it was. Maybe they'll have to be connected again, no matter how different paths they have chosen. The separation was easy because they got busy in their own lives, they both made a tiny world around them.

Chanda with her offline friends that physically presents with her. Here Madhu with her fandom social media friend circle. Side by side they both were exploring new hobbies and interests, like Chanda was doing for

YouTube MVs and Madhu is editing for the fanpage, they already felt the beginning of the future life path. At least they started to feel the rise of the ARTIST self lies in their soul, they already got to realise they're not pursuing anything with their academics. But the vision was still blurry about what they're actually going to do. Lockdown was the time period where THEY found THEMSELVES. They met their soul.

As I said previously, Lockdown was a blessing , at least for them, they had learnt a lot, explored a lot that's what made their trembling steps more stable and strong.

EXPLORING

"Meeting your soul who's lost within"

~ Madhurima

It is one of the best experiences one could ever have in this human lifetime, by finding their true self again, that makes someone feel free and fulfilled.

DON'T LET THE RETROGRADE
LEAVE YOU FRAYED.
TAKE CARE OF YOURSELF!

"Exploring" or "Explore" means *"Talaash"* in Hindi, that means to find something. But why is this chapter entitled like this, what were they trying to explore. They were finding nothing but their own selves. Their inner-self was finding their soul to know their life purpose. And this *"Talaash"* made them try a lot of new things. I'm pretty sure that y'all also been there in your life at least once. While running the fanpage, Madhu tried a bunch of hobbies as a career option like sketching, shayaris, Insta page, YouTube, Editing and so on. Chanda went for a free entrepreneur course, singing, fashion designing, event management and modelling but deep inside she wanted to be an actress. All these gave them some experiences. They tried so much in the lockdown period so that's why people love their career counselling ,because they know how exactly to do what you want.

They gained experience but that time, experience isn't enough. Their soul is seeking some magic and in 2 months of 2020 the magic began to Spark. The MAGIC upon which this book is based. We all do have MAGIC within, that MAGIC is the very essence of our life and now that began to unfold.

Madhu made up her mind that she wanna be a filmmaker and she is going with editing first. Chanda also decided without any weaver that she's going to pursue her acting career. And you know this one decision is what actually matters. We always have a choice and a decision to make. And you have to dream big irrespective of the situations you are seeing around, and unknowingly they did that. They saw the vision of what they want to experience in this life, something great something wonderful and surreal. And that's the moment when Magic started to happen. The last two phases are all about how manifestation came into these two late teenagers lives and changed everything for enlightenment.

Relationship can't be owned by just a single person, if one gets busy or not putting any efforts then it is not possible that only one person is going to survive that relation alone .

But what happened with these two because they had enough time for each other thanks to lockdown. It's not like they totally locked the door of heart they still talk to each other, it's just that old spark vanished somewhere. And what tragic is they both were unaware about that fact. If we think now about like such kind of moment had between us in past or if we tell somebody , no one's going to believe but we realized & believe too that it was necessary for our growth , for our bond.

Krishna always teaches us in his way and we learnt in our way. Although there was time where we believe that it's our fault. Even if is Madhu's fake case of cyber crime or Chanda's infatuation on unwanted circumstances.

Okay... we were learning a lot by those situations of our life. That period of lockdown is became our base of strength. we made mistakes but at the end of the day we learnt from that.

There is saying that "The darkest hour of night is just before of sunrise"

The lockdown period was that "darkest hour" for us and for others too. We were exploring ourselves, in terms of emotion, our knowledge , our talents and also we were learning new things. With addition of pain, pain of losing time, pain of losing love, pain of not getting notice from our idol.

In lockdown we were actually understand the value of nature and mother earth, we're inhaling oxygen in free that's a big deal if look into it. We had not big task to do in our homes because of that we were focusing on every little details of life like. "How it feels when wind touches your body & soul, talking to moon , witnessing sunset & Autumn"

Thanks to lockdown we started to understand and we got time to feel actually all of these. Where news channel was killing our hope , Mother nature was holding our hand.Love without expectation. that's the thing Chanda felt the most .

She's a practical girl she knows that she deserves to be happy . but she had a question about life & love that gained in lockdown . Both Madhu & Chanda never liked to gain sympathy from anyone like why all of these happened to us?? They both have curious soul to find an answer of all the weird questions regarding life. 2020 is ending and new journey takes place in their story which was about

Spirituality & Laws Of Life. Beginning Of Magic.

Universal Gift

According to Divine Law of Oneness "We all are interconnected through our creation by creator"

That means everything that exist in this world , no one actually have anything and everyone have everything in this materialistic world. Just time to time owners changes !!

What we desire it already exists in this world , some souls are might be experiencing this . As we all are connected you can experience your desire too through your imagination , you can imagine because it is already here in this world.

When Chanda was in hometown she decides that when she go back in Mumbai, she's going to take admission in Acting class. Impatient she, She called the one of Acting about Procedure & Fee. Receptionist received and told her everything. When she get to know about Fee , she felt that she couldn't arrange that much amount but her burning desire was to take admission in that class. After 6 months she came back , she planned that she's going to do Job for fee but within 3 days she got her job too but doing job wasn't her desire , she never wants to do Job.

In lunch time she called again in that Class after seeing a post that new batch going to start soon although she knows that she didn't have Fee right now. Class's Owner who's teacher also of that class , he received her call and agreed to give her scholarship of 50% discount. She don't know how she gets but she gets what's she actually wants.

We don't have to look on, how ?? we just need to tell our Desire to Universe.

AWAKENING

2020
2021
2022
— DANICA GIM

IS THIS REAL ?

DOOR

OPENING

"There's thousands of ways

In which one you're going to stay

You're the master of your fate.

let's open the fairy world's gate."

~ Chanda

There's a saying of Martin Luther "only in the darkness can you see the stars."

The lockdown period was full of darkness for everyone and for both too. But if we see , the lockdown gave everyone a chance to know themselves and it was a blessing to everyone by mother earth and knowing the Law of attraction was the STAR in darkness for both. According to them lockdown could be defined as "A black ball made up of all colours", not everyone can recognize except the one who has an eye to observe and learn. Fortunately these two have that. They got introduced by the laws of life, kind of reality of life. Every human deserves to get to know about it and the universe gives everyone equal opportunity to know. Everyone's appointed time is different and it was their time to acknowledge the law, apply it in life and get what they truly deserve and be the best version of themselves.

CHANDA'S POV

Is this real ?

So many questions filled my mind. I was familiar with tarot cards and had a keen interest in astrology. At that time, I wasn't aware that such predictions were readily available and quite general. I believed only priests could determine destiny through palmistry and Grah-vastu. However, the idea of sending "Love Vibrations" was new and intriguing to me..

Desperately, without understanding the core principles, I followed video instructions. Of course, nothing happened. Looking back, I realize I was acting out of lack: lack of knowledge, lack of confidence, and lack of self-love. I was an unhealed person trying to send out positive vibrations, but I was met with the same energy of "lack." Around that time, I also lost one of my close friends, which deeply affected me as I felt I was constantly losing people. Despite these challenges, I believe that "everything happens for a reason." This negative period led me to a video about "Energy," where I learned how energy transforms and operates..

Exactly, not just in Newtonian physics, but everything, including us and our surroundings, is made of nothing but "ENERGY." That's how our universe functions. A slight smile crossed my face, knowing her soul was now free. I bid her a final goodbye from my side, confident that she would always be there for me. All these experiences converged, leading me to delve deeper into the fundamental "Laws" of Life.

I came across the "Law of Attraction," but initially, I struggled with it. The techniques and methods seemed almost like witchcraft, and it was challenging to accept. Despite my reservations, I found myself trying it out. My YouTube algorithm kept suggesting similar videos one after another. While it was popular online, it didn't seem like everyone was using it to manifest their desires in real life. I felt a strong desire to talk about and share it, but uncertainty held me back. When we're unsure about something, it's natural to hesitate sharing it with others.

If any of you are experiencing what I did, know that you'll find your partner soon. When we manifest true knowledge and wisdom, we naturally attract someone to share and discuss it with, just like I manifested Madhu. She's now my first successful manifestation. In truth, everything in my life, even rejection, has been my own creation. I don't regret any of it; every experience has taught me resilience and propelled me towards personal growth and development.

MADHU'S POV

As you already read that Chanda was finding answers in Tarot and Witchy stuffs. And me ?! I literally had found something I could call "Magic" back then. It was something many of you possibly know, it was subliminal. I actually used to work-out too hard, and I followed so many health influencers on social media. There was a channel named "Nimesha", this girl is the first one who introduced me to the subliminal stuff. The very first subliminal I heard, was for height increase but I gave up after one listen, LMAO. Lack of knowledge you know. But unknowingly I actually opened the doorway to my upgraded life which I had dreamt of. So after that I literally got surrounded by everything that led me to know about the Universal laws or especially LAW OF ATTRACTION. This term is really famous and so many people are having a lot of success with it, but it was something that's the primary stage of my journey. Knowing about this was the manifestation itself, as we all know that we have been manifesting throughout our whole goddamn life. So yeah, now my focus had been shifted from fandom toxicity to my own personal development. That's really good because it's just the beginning of my journey. I started binge watching manifestation videos, various coaches and reading posts online and all this was changing me a lot. All of this seemed something like "woo-woo" and like "magic" to me back then, I wasn't also fully believing all of these. Many of you who have been on this journey of self exploration are getting me right now, which changes I'm talking about.

So much love for y'all who are on the beginning stage now or not started their journey yet, don't worry love, you deserve it. Anytime, even when you're reading this, you're gonna get there. You already have everything, trust me everything in this world is yours. I hope I could believe all these back then. Whatever, everyone has their own story of getting into this self exploration or manifestation journey. This is mine, like so many or unlike everyone. Subliminal had brought me to the manifestation community.

So this is how Chanda and Madhu had found the bridge. The bridge that connects two versions of them, the current one and the best one. Now they have to take steps to walk the bridge. There was fog, there was blurry vision, there was lack of clarity but one thing they had gotten is the Courage to take the steps. And both of them managed to start walking, because there was no other way. They had already dreamt of their best lives. And it's the only thing or the last thing I could say they should do in order to get their dreams.

Now the journey had become much more interesting. Their story now started taking the twist and leap of faith.

Now not only them , we are all gonna walk the bridge with them. There are turbulence, drastic changes, and a flood of emotions, becoming completely different, and why not! After all we're shifting realities. As we are exploring our true self, our souls.

They already got into the rollercoaster and tightened their grips. Let's go. Enjoy the ride of self exploration, wisdom and learning.

Confessing

The LAW

"We confessed together

we entered in the fairy world together

we were there together

we're here together"

~ Chanda

Madhu and Chanda were screaming at the top of their voices, jumping like an animal, punching on their beds. The happiness they had at that moment is quite indescribable. And you already know the reason, don't you!?

They just got to know that they both started believing in something, yeah that's the law of attraction. And they didn't even know that they were in the same boat.

It was 3rd February, 2021. Madhu knew that chanda wasn't satisfied with her life and a lil bit disturbed with her shitty people around her. That's why Madhu decided to explain Chanda about the law, It didn't matter to her if Madhu didn't know and understand the law completely at that point. She's always ready to teach the other one. Like bro, first go and learn it , then teach it to others. But nah, she's always in her leader attitude.

So she wasn't aware that Chanda also knew the laws. But when the atoms collided, a force called "Exchange interaction" arises, and that's kind of chaotic. The same happened when Madhu told Chanda about the law, Chanda got overwhelmed by joy that now she had someone to talk about the stuffs, she was learning lately. And Madhu began to tell her with a hesitant voice but now she's equally overwhelmed that now she can discuss everything with her. Because we all know when we really have to learn something we have to discuss it over, over and over again. And after having 18 years of subconscious programming of this limited society, in this 3d world, it's really not easy for someone to walk that bridge alone, at least it was not for them. So from then we had started walking together but not holding each other's hands tightly. This is also our own personal journey from 'walking together but distant' to 'glued each other's hands really tight'. And this day was also the fresh start of our bond, we started walking as STRANGERS to SOUL SISTERS again.

STRANGERS TO SOUL SISTERS

Self
Mastery

"The universe gave us this mortal body to know the immortal soul. For soul freedom we must disciple our body"

~ Chanda

Self mastery is simply learning to think, learning to listen to our intuition, learning to feel all the emotions that exist, except the negative one, but when it comes to something negative instead of worrying or suppressing that emotion, just feel it. Analyze it. Why do I feel like this? then make yourself free of it. Learning to do what you have decided, learning to communicate without thought of being judged , learning to lead your own life , and learning to be yourselves . It is simple but not easy because of our ongoing programming of the conscious mind since childhood.

In the journey of mastery on self we encountered lots of things and all of these things, we will tell you in detail but yes that process makes us believe and realise the core truth and knowledge of what the universe is trying to teach us. It was happening because somewhere our soul wanted to be free , and our dreams wanna fly .

Maybe you all know this dialogue from "Om Shanti Om"

"Itni Shiddat se maine tumhe paane ki koshish ki hai, ke har zarre ne mujhe tumse Milane ki saazish ki hai. Kehte hain ki...agar kisi cheez ko dil se chaaho to puri kayanat usey tumse milane ki koshish mein lag jaati hai"

GRATEFULNESS

Well well well, thank you so much buddy that you're with us till now, grateful we are. Yes, that gratefulness is from our very core of heart. But just 2 years ago, we just don't know how to be grateful in our life and not to complain about things. "Being grateful" is the very first thing that everyone has to practice in this journey.

Initially we have to practice gratitude for all the things we have, even the smallest one, and not only things but also the people we have. Everything good we have in our lives, we should be grateful. Even for the negative things because they've taught us something in order to fix the mistakes and grow in life by not repeating the same. That's how this manifestation community teaches you to be grateful. And it's really great and feels really good and relaxes your goddamn monkey minds. So as y'all did, Me and Chanda also started practicing gratitude. And it really helps us to build the core foundations of this journey. After a certain point of time this has become on auto pilot. Now we don't intentionally be grateful to our wishes, it comes automatically.

At the beginning it's kinda annoying for sceptical minds, that how could one be grateful about the things they don't even have. But we have to because if we have the desire, we have the thing too. That's how we should pray or claim our desires. I got you besties, we've been there too. But believe me on this one, that in this vast multiverse you have all of your desires and living the best version of your life. And we just shift realities one to another among the infinite realities. We promise that at the end of this book you're really gonna have the vivid idea of reality shifting, it's so legitimately possible and you can do it too.

PAYING GRATITUDE

How do we pay gratitude to someone??

By saying "Thank you" right!

When we say thank you to anyone or god or universe that means you have something and you value it . And the sense of " having " is necessary for your consciousness because then it provides satisfaction to you. Younger Madhu and Chanda didn't know about it, like how important it is to feel grateful for what you have first, then you demand the next. The thought " I wish I had it , why don't I have this ? why am I here ? ". All of these questions and complaints about situations show you're not happy and satisfied with your current situation and the universe says "you have to feel grateful".

Because what you have right now, is somewhere in this world someone's wish . You just can't disrespect it so easily and one more thing, among all of these things that you own, basically you haven't earned it , you're gifted and provided by someone else or we can say universe.

Why are you not happy??

SELF LOVE

If we have to explain self love in one line then we would say "Choosing yourself first or making yourselves a priority, isn't being selfish ". Self love is simply like, you treat yourself same as like you treat your loved ones. There's a thin line between self love and being rude to someone and guys here's a crystal clear truth.

" You can only love someone when you first love yourself" because self love teaches us basically how to love , when you prioritise yourself you know about yourself more , like "why you're feeling this emotion at this time" and that helps to understand someone else better .

When we're in full of love - we attract love ,

When we're in lack of love - we attract lack .

Most people don't understand this simple method , instead of realising or analysis they just complain , "no one loves me , I'm not a priority of someone , my friends ignore me all the time , they just contact me when they need me" cut the crap mannn !!!.

This complaining and all are just bullshit

Why are you not getting " why will someone make you priority , did you make yourself a priority?? "

No right ??

Then how can you expect others to treat you like you wanted to be treated. And first of all why do people just wait for others like "someone will come and she/he makes me feel special".

Ohh darling and young man love yourself first saying these things about self love is so easy now. But back then Madhu and Chanda!! they were also in lack of love, they just knew to love others without expecting but they didn't love themselves first, and there they both lacking and law of attraction gradually teaches them "you two stupid girls love yourself first"

The universe is a good teacher, you know.

MEDITATION

There's a big taboo between teenagers like "Meditation is only for old people or people who are in their 40's & 50's , Why do we do meditation we aren't monks or saints."

I know not every teenager reacts like this but most of the...

We have seen this kind of people in our colleges , they like to worry about everything and pray to god "God ! god ! please don't do that not now"

But when we advise them "do meditation and start practicing to calm your mind" they just laugh or smirk and forget .

Guys we can do meditation anywhere or at any age of life .

What is meditation??

Meditation is basically awareness, awareness about your thoughts and body and current state of mind.

There's a simple difference between meditation and prayer "when we pray to the god we're actually saying to them about our problems and when we do meditate we're listening to God". God is within ourselves , your inner intuition is your God .

Power of meditation, Madhu understood before Chanda , but meditation was the only thing that helped them both in calming their minds .

• To give importance to actual positive feelings rather than any kind of negativity.

• To know about inner thought.

• To be aware of everything that runs in your mind.

• Live in the moment , helps to stop worrying about the future and the past.

• It teaches us to be patient

There's much more actually what we got by just doing meditation.

Both authors are advising you guys to MEDITATE even for just 5min. It will help you a lot in your respective areas of life

WE PROMISE.

METHODS

Methods are trap or scary at the same time

I mean if you don't write 573924 times your manifestation will not come true.

This technique works in 7 days , this works faster, this method will change your life.

Sounds weird right ? It is weird actually but initially like people who have just been introduced by the law of attraction, they might be fall in these kind of titled videos on youtube and we both too fallen in these traps of methods. Because instead of gaining wisdom of law we were doing this technique to get our desire

And if you don't understand the law these techniques are never gonna work out. Your actual technique and method is your subconscious mind, that's the key. If you don't believe in what you're writing then of course it will not going to manifest. At the end of the day only believe & faith are going to work for you.

We're not against these techniques, we both agree that these techniques actually help to impress your subconscious but only if you believe. But it doesn't mean if methods say "you have to write your desire at this time, if you fail to maintain that time then it means you're making some mistake and you are not going to get your desires." Blah blah blah!!! When people get afraid, that is the scary part of techniques we were talking about .

We don't have to be afraid of our desires.

MARVEL

Madhu always came up with some marvellous things which helped us to understand the law and quantum physics in an easy way and that is none other than " MARVEL CINEMATIC UNIVERSE "

Yayyyyyyyy !!!! Yeah you heard it right. We heard about superheroes like iron man, captain America, Hulk, spiderman and Superman (oops) LoL, but we hadn't watched all those more than amazing movies and series, we really don't know that what the fuck we were doing all our teenage years. But maybe it had to happen right after we started our manifestation journey. We can never deny the fact that Marvel played a crucial role in engraving our beliefs. Our Marvel marathon was such a fun along with the learnings. We have to mention the Doctor Strange movies here especially the first one. "OMFG" that's the reaction when we first watched it, the whole movie is based on the theories, we binge watch on YouTube and read in this manifestation community. Stan Lee had literally written all the mystery of the universe in his comics.

These contents helped to understand the multiverse theory, quantum realm, time and space etc. All together Marvel had taught us a lot about how the universal laws work. And we want to add one more that besides these Marvel characters inspired us to be great, how to be limitless, how to be powerful, how to be confident af, how to be a badass, to be the best version of ourselves, how to be a good soul and more which added value to our lives. So in a nutshell Marvel turned us into superheroes too.

So we got marvel , marvel got some new admirers. Especially
Chanda and Madhu got each other , our bond had
developed not only with time but watching marvel and
learning together.

COACHES

The interesting thing is we never went to get any private coaching. But we listened to so many of them online like y'all do. And we're the living testimonials that if you have a learning mindset you can learn from every-fucking-where, like we did. So as we never did coaching with some particular individual but we had to stick with one coach back then. The first person we had learnt the law of attraction , was Master Sri Akarshana. He's really famous and probably most of you know him. But after a few months, we needed to upgrade because change was needed and all that knowledge was not seeming enough to us. Then we found someone who taught us further, and she is Anjana Ma'am known as Anjana Reetoria. She actually taught us how to treat the universe, how to wish like a child, how to manifest by just asking the universe. Also there are so many manifestation coaches, we had listened but we never stick to them more than one week max to max. These two are the longest. Then we baid the good bye to Law of Attraction, because we need more upgradation.

This is how we, two late teenagers were trembling in self mastery while maintaining our day to day 3d life, otherwise general non-awakened people around were gonna call us freaks. However we still just stayed there for a while and then literally started manifesting randomly, that made us believe more in all these.

Started

Manifesting

It takes a lot of courage to take responsibility of our every manifestation, either wanted or unwanted.

~ Madhurima

Marvel teaches us "Great power comes with great responsibility" but the thing is power never comes. It is already within you. You have to just realise "The Youniverse in YOU" and then boom. That's what happened to us, after realising the manifestation stuff, we were actually doing *Man-maani* kind of thing. But just like there's a difference between knowledge & wisdom. Same here, there is actually difference between knowing and then after realising how much you trained yourself to see good in everything and everyone fucking situation of life. Because now you're trying to change yourself according to your new perspective, then what about your surroundings?? They're still the same and you have to deal with them without being bursted, just by using your presence of mind. You don't even know how much power your mind possesses, because how we react in any situation matters, most of the decision making in life. If you guys don't want to regret , just be, live in the moment to analyse what the fuck is going on in your life and it's time to fix it no matter how but we have to, like

"Pick your broken *Heart* and turn it into *Art*"

If something goes wrong , still you're not changed to your upgraded version right !? , you can turn the table anytime. You can start now to change.

People might think "It's a thing that only looks good in books or novels, real life scenarios are different."

No guys, Madhu and Chanda can be the biggest example for you like we're here from nowhere. But in this journey of course we fail at first we will tell you in our POVs.

CHANDA'S POV

As I told you before, how I was stuck in my hometown but it's okay , no regrets ! Because I guess it had to happen for my betterment, most precious months of my life where I had learnt a lot of things and practiced gratitude & writing , realised the core knowledge , watched marvel etc. Those months universe gifted me , otherwise if I had not gone to my hometown then I would have stayed in Mumbai and tried to find hundreds of ways to reach the goal but I had never stuck to none of them. I'm glad and grateful that universe bought some time for me and my soul. In those times I started manifesting.

I know every second of life , situation , relationship , incident , is manifested by me but that conscious manifesting was actually started from my hometown. Like I could eat whatever, whenever I want, yes I manifested a lot of food items in my hometown where it was really difficult to get those foods because the market was far more than you could imagine. People who had hard feelings for me , they ended up liking me and praising me. I guess the most important thing that I manifested that time is , I started to live in the present because I'm kinda person who freaks out a lot by just thinking of career. Why I'm wasting my time etc. Because who I am, wherever I am, successful or not at the end of the day it's just me , I started to accept myself .

I actually fell in love with myself.

MADHU'S POV

Same as Chanda, me also started having vivid vision about my career, what exactly makes me happy, what I wanted to do. Things became more clearer as I was growing forward with baby steps. But my one of the most beautiful manifestation is when I realised, that person I loved, my twinsoul is already mine. We're already together, we have our own fairytale dream life together. That realisation never fades away, so my love is. I was always like " he's mine, I'm his, no ifs no buts, we are eternally together before this human life". That time all the fear evaporated somewhere and never touched me again.

Learning From Our Mistakes

"Mistakes made us realize us our power"

Because if we can create that much mess so we can create that much beauty too. It's all within ourselves, our minds.

~ Madhurima

THIS TOO SHALL PASS
AND YOU WILL APPRECIATE LIFE MORE THAN EVER BEFORE
@DREAMY_MOONS

Let me clear here one thing which is you'll know very well that no one is perfect, and doing mistake is totally 'okayyyy' & normal. Mistakes show that you're trying to do at least and we believe that "FAILURE" word doesn't exist. Basically, they are lessons of life, if we took success as a gift from universe or god then failure is must be the lessons to improve ourselves much better, like be the best version of ourselves.

We're not Doctor Strange who never learns from his mistakes. We're Tony Stark right? Who always learns from his mistakes and most importantly he never repeats those mistakes.

We know you all are might be thinks why author suddenly saying about mistakes. Actually here's a thing that "sometimes it is hard to fight with the 18 years old programming of mind until we became totally healed person" in journey of conscious manifestation. Some of the wishes were fulfilled so easily in just one blink of an eye but some of them were taking time. Do you know why ???? Because .....

Not believing The Universal Laws

We believed at first, but we didn't actually believe in like we were testing and trying. We were let's just try what will happen if we think like in this way or that way, we treat & act like something magic going to happen. But it is not a magic right, that was the reason we were unable to get what we desire. Chanda was a science student and Madhu loves to read article based on physics. Later that thing helped us in comprehension the law.

Practice makes perfect but wrong practice will not make you perfect

We had realised really soon that there was 'something off' in us, something really we were missing out on. Then we started to search about Law of attraction and our algorithm of Youtube & Instagram had caught. We started to learn from various coaches, we used to read on posts, we read *N* number of post on daily basis, on theory basis we collected a lot of data in our mind but when it had to be done in practical, except lil things we were unable to manifest.

It's just we consumed a lot, we can explain anyone very clearly but practically possibilities and theoretical knowledge , these are different things right . later we just stopped to looking guidance in social media posts and started to read books based on laws.

Meditation & Laws hate desperation

We already told you guys about the importance of meditation but being honest here, we do not meditate even after knowing. that led us in desperation every time a question pop up in mind " why nothing is happening ??, we're doing everything correctly" & due to our desperate energy we used to calculate everything.

"Aisa Kiya, toh aisa hoga, isse ye milega, kya galat ho gaya", basically habits of looking for 'HOW', that we don't have to do. and also we believe in law but we just don't believe in ourselves or in our desire or end result.

when we were just consuming the law on theoretical basis ,
a realisation hits hard that our mind and heart aren't align
to each other. For their alignment we have to do meditation.

Grateful for everything but not truly

Like if we are being grateful for what we have in morning
and rest of the day counting what we don't have then what
our Subconscious will absorb ??

Of course It will count "Lack" because we all know
subconscious is always working 24/7 .

We need to understand , we need to be aware about our
thoughts , when you're busy in something then what's going
on back of the head .

Awareness is the key to know more about ourselves.
Whenever you feel you don't have what you truly desire
then just show your mind you always got what you wanted
once .

Being in moment but wait do you actually understand what it truly means?

Living in present, be in the moment, what does it mean ?

it means enjoy the present wherever you are without
worrying about future but in teenage life the habit of always
thinking about future was not going to cure so easily until or
unless we actually found a way of our dream.

Like Chanda decides when she will come Mumbai , she'll
join Acting class because having talent is good but it should

be shaped beautifully and teachers can only guide in best way.

Let your subconscious find a way for your all dreams and desires. You just need to follow your intuition and you will understand the difference between random thoughts and intuition when you are stays in present moment.

Don't need to panic always sometimes just go with the flow

Krishna says *"Tu karm karte jaa, phal ki chinta na kar"* means we just need to do our work , if you can't able to think good then don't think negative also just let it be .

like Madhu wasn't so much into career kind of thing but in this journey she realises her dream , she always likes to edit videos later she decided to make this as career and she need to be fully trained , like how actually things works in post production. Suddenly one day Madhu called Chanda

She said while crying *"Hum na apni friendship khatam karte hai, kyu ki ismein koi scope nahi hai."*

That time Chanda got worried why she's suddenly saying all of this things. She first calmed her then asked what happened??

Madhu replied "I was searching editing institute but every institute is fake , how I'll learn and how I'm going to come Mumbai, I can't find any way"

But you know what guys after just few days like a magic she found a trusted institute in Kolkata and her family agreed for her joining.

Panicking about any situation is not going to help in anyway. Consistency is so fucking important. Letting go of desire is good but 'Let go' in a positive way always works but if you think like you can't manifest this now and forget your desire then it will not going to show up in your reality , consistency is so important . Not being consistent brings dwelling in our thoughts basically. If we put laws aside , normally dwelling in life is not good , we need to choose one always.

Universe (Subconscious) reads energy , in which energy you stays all days. And Living in wish fulfilment is the best way to trick our mind.

These are mistakes we were done in our manifestation & growing journey , though we never regret , because everytime we had learned so much and it's okay to do mistakes in life because those mistakes makes you perfect , Your imperfection is your true beauty , and never hesitate on your mistakes at least you tried , God always helps those who helps themselves. If you believe than everything is true.

These are our mistakes your can be something else which is not mentioned here. It's okay to do to mistakes , you have to do just one thing Always learn from them.

Hashtag normalise to do MISTAKES.

So basically learning from mistakes is

• Be the Tony stark not Doctor Strange

• Do believe in yourself , what you know , others don't know

• Sometimes you don't have to know everything , never consume more than enough

• Be master in practically not just theoretically

• Don't have to look "How" it's not your job

• Do Meditation only for 5 min but start from today

• Be grateful for what you have

• Be in the moment

• Time has all the answers , just go with the flow

• Never question on your desire , if you have desire then it meant to be yours

• Be consistence

• Learn from books rather than social media

• Love yourself first

Universe Brought Us Together

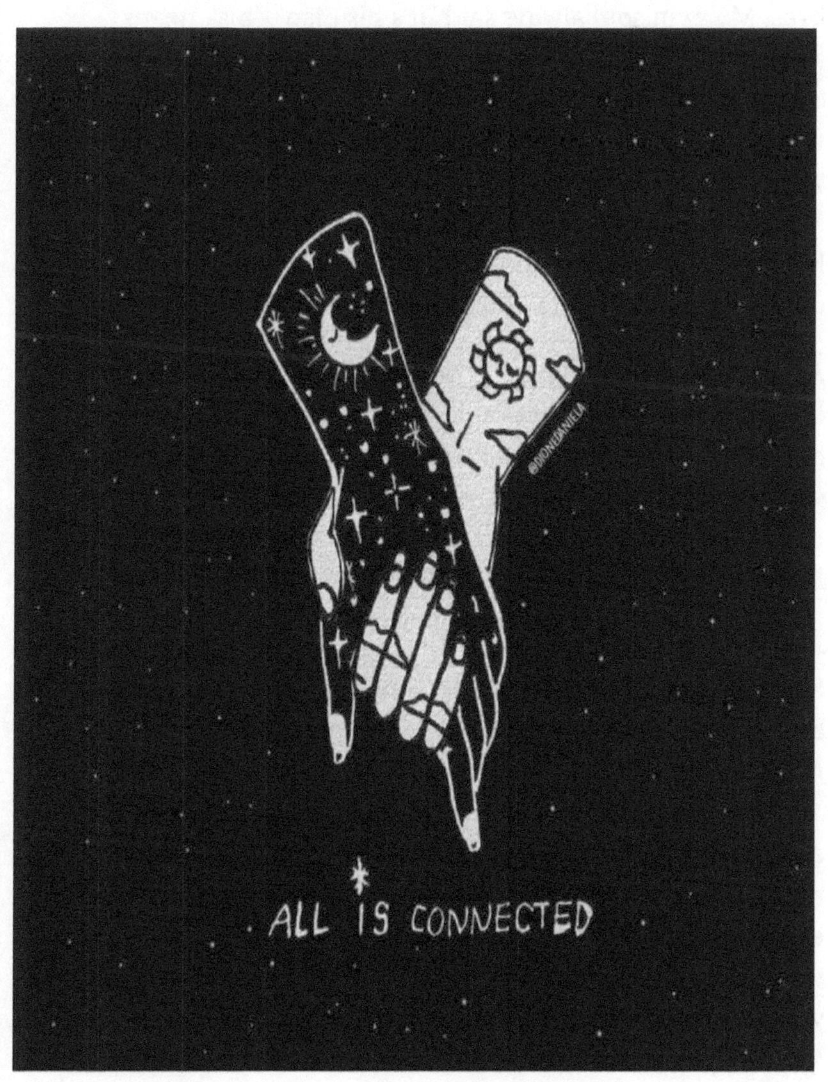

ALL IS CONNECTED

Heyy besties, Madhu is here.....

"Universe brought us together" this line just justified our lives. My twin soul always said "it's his plan", 'his' means some greater energy or we can call it 'Universe'. As the chapter name said the universe brought us together. It really was. As it was already the beginning months of 2022 and we were already in this journey of Manifesting our true selves. Now Me and Chanda were walking together but this time holding each other's hands so tightly, like a forever bond, unbreakable and made of nothing but LOVE.

As we were still juggling a lil but now we were used to it. All that turbulence became stable. And for some sudden decision I had to shift to a PG. I got an internship, but that was the worst one. Also some changes happened in my day to day life. But as I said everything is in a plan. I stayed in PG for maybe a month, then I decided to quit that internship and get back to my place.

So in the last week there on my room bed I was laying down and for the very first time I saw a post about "Shifting realities", and that seemed interesting to me. I read the post and sent it straight to Chanda. Fortunately my Instagram algorithm caught that, and started showing me the same posts, that's how new gateways were becoming clearer than ever. We got to know about Neville Goddard, one of the greatest law of assumption teachers. And with Neville's words we stepped in to a new journey, with more advanced knowledge of Manifesting. And this one is also backed up with science that is why we have learnt the law more intensely, from it's core. We gained knowledge every aspect of universal laws. And all these made our way to the Enlightenment phase of our life as well as of this book.

The Most Beautiful Bond Ever Of our life that we have each other as a friend, bestie, soul-sister. Just a casual friend to soul sister, we have lived this journey together.

It's not made of in one day relationship or based on only one situation , It's a journey of 5 years togetherness , Lil cat fights , not hearing each other's perspective to understands each other as a person.

It's not happened because of only one person in this relationship, we both understood our assignment very well for each other. Although we never had that much idea at the beginning that we will going to stay together till the end and going to make our decade happen together.

We all have heard about online dating and Love stories but ours is Friendship story that makes us special. It all started in back 2018 , Universe always have the great plan for everyone and Universe gave "US" & "WE4".

We Can share our every little thought to our biggest plan , Every achievement to every embarrassing story , and we listen to each other that's without any judgement. We praise each other but if there's something wrong we never hasitate to point out our mistakes. The level of comfort we have, couldn't be described in words.

SOUL SISTERS

One thing for sure we never forced something in our friendship. It just happened like it's pre-planned

Because We Know Universe brought us together , Blessed by our higher selves.

The things I wanna mention that seems like a blessing to me ,Madhurima.

The most impressive manifestation of mine is "I cured my PCOD/PCOS."

Medical research said that PCOS isn't curable we just can control it by lifestyle changes and maintaining a good hormonal balance. But I denied my PCOD in my reality, I command to have a healthy reproduction system, normal hormonal balance and regular menstrual cycle. And My subconscious followed the command and did the rest.

I firmly believe that nature listens to me. That's how I controlled weather. Again my command came in. I manifested rain, sunny days, even denied a cyclone and it happened according to my command. Can you guys realise how much power your words and mind have ?

There are a lot more things in day to day life that I have manifested with my commands. I make everything count, because when I became aware of my thoughts, I became the queen of my reality. The reality is at my command, I became a deliberate creator.

ENLIGHTENMENT

MY REALITY iS
CREATED BY ME

UNIVERSAL

LAWS

"Not all the Laws are meant to bind, Some are meant to be give us freedom to think beyond this body and material world"

~ Chanda

YOU ARE
AN EXTENSION
OF THE
UNIVERSE
ITSELF

Our UNIVERSE as an individual one or as part of this vast multiverse operates based on some of its own principles. And all these laws aren't biased. It works for everyone on the same level. All of these are here to be used by everyone, every soul that is incarnated in this 3d world. And the one who wins, is the one who's able to do their self mastery. And as soon as we realised this universal fact, our consciousness snapped in. This is really a tricky fact to stay awakened in this illusionary holographic universe, which is continuously moving, changing and fluctuating according to our minds.

We all are given one mind as a remote control to operate not only in this 3d world but also the super world also known as the quantum realm or 4d reality. The conscious part operates the 3d and the subconscious part operates the 4d, as simple as that. This is the very base knowledge in this manifestation community. But Madhu and Chanda never read all those non-fiction books before, that's why they didn't have access to all these. They only got to know what Instagram and Youtubers told them. That is why it took a little longer for them to get there.

Well well well, that one post about shifting realities (mentioned before) changes everything. As a Marvel fan they both have a very deep understanding about the multiverse concept, because they both are very much interested in. And it is the very core key, how we manifest things. So that post made them think how they were going to shift there, to their desired one. And as we all know every question comes with its answers. There's no answer if there's not a question about it. So they started reading more of the posts related to it and somehow someway they actually stepped out of that zone of law of attraction and stepped into the zone of "Universal laws" that includes everything.

There are so many other keys that help us to be the best versions of ourselves, like self concept, confidence, becoming Love, not fearing anything, forgiveness, stick to your decision and last but not the least 3d reality is dead and so on. Now they have more things to work on, to learn, to change, to become. Become whatever they want to. They stopped binge reading posts and watching YouTube videos about laws and manifestations. They started to claim now, claim something as theirs, with confidence and authority. As we all should. And this is how situations started to change for all the best and beautiful.

Chanda and Madhu are like each other's mentors. They both teach each other, they both learn from every-fucking-where. Now according to their understanding, let's explain the perspective of these two old souls in these 20 year old bodies.

When they got the way, all that chaos of excessive knowledge started to fade away. And they started to learn the very core and authenticity of Universal laws. Madhu and Chanda have that key now, the key to manifest, is nothing but reality shifting that we all are simultaneously doing according to our dominant thoughts. For all those very sceptical minds, like you guys have a hard time believing in these stuffs, so we can say it's all in our subconscious mind(95%of our brain), this part or our mind is the vehicle that very remote, which helps to shift from one reality to another that exists parallel in the quantum realm or world. What does that mean!? that means all of your wishes, dreams, your best and worst life versions, everything you could possibly imagine, every fucking tiny possibilities exist there. We choose where we are going or staying for a moment by choosing and by our thoughts. And the rest of the work done by our subconscious mind, it knows how to shift your whole existence to an another reality. As we all are just made of energy, like we are energy waves that bundled together to make a figure that supports to love in this 3d World. And all those things you can see around you in this world are just energies transformed in a shape to exist in this earth. So that we all can feel them with our five senses that operated by our 5% of mind (conscious mind). Long story short, we are always shifting according to our thoughts, that we do believe in, that could be desirable or also could be so problematic and unfavourable.

This human life is a game of beliefs, if you do believe in something one hundred percent without a single shadow of a doubt, your subconscious mind takes it as an order and does the rest. Same as when you order something online, your order will gonna definitely delivered to you. There you spend money and here you spend thoughts and "focused attention" as your currency.

There's not a single law, like that famous and overrated "LAW OF ATTRACTION", that governs the whole multiverse. Nah besties! There are laws and they all work out for everyone's favour who believes wholeheartedly and people who don't even know, the laws work out for them too according to their dominant thoughts . Let's take a glance at those.

• Law of divine oneness: We are all connected.

• Law of vibration: Each particle in the Universe is made of energy.

• Law of action: To achieve something, one must take action (PS: we can say inspired action that's required to get there in your desired one)

• Law of correspondence: Outer world is a reflection of our inner world.

• Law of attraction: Like attracts like.

• Law of cause and effect: You get back whatever you send into universe.

• Law of compensation: You get as good as you give

• Law of perpetual transmutation of energy: The universe keeps changing

• Law of relativity: Every individual is tested by the universe.

• Law of rhythm: Everything goes through cycles/rhythm/pattern

• Law of polarity: Everything in universe has an opposite

• Law of gender: All things have masculine & feminine components.

Hey hey !! Don't freak out. You don't have to learn all of those to get what you want, you already have all your desires in different realities. But if you do know about these laws

,that also helps to grow. There are also "seven hermetic principles", these are so much ancient evidence of Universal laws and mysteries. Manifestation is not a **woo woo** trendy internet topic, it's a lifestyle. Our whole life is a manifestation. It has been there since a very ancient time. But somehow when society and normal basic science started to evolve, we all humans had forgotten the importance of teaching these laws and mastering our own selves.

As we already mentioned before, Madhu and Chanda walked a lot of different roads to know exactly how this "manifestation" works, because they also had a hard time believing that all of these are real, until they got the understanding themselves. It's something like the answers of their every question were provided by the infinite intelligence, whenever a query appeared, the answer automatically appeared too in its own ways. All of it takes so much time and effort. But yeah it all is the part of their journey to go through it. You guys do your own research, that really helps in subconscious programming but we don't want you guys to also be stuck in those tips, tricks, hacks and methods that this manifestation community teaches. So that's why we're mentioning "REALITY SHIFTING" the actual core concept of manifestation (according to our beliefs). This is also backed up and based on quantum theory, multiverse concept and how your subconscious mind operates. There are so many Books available, go and read from authentic sources that let you know everything you need to. And in this book we are also gonna give you something that helps us to manifest and surely going to help y'all too.

DECADE

PLANNING

"The thread, that connects souls, is made of Love. Even one string could be torn but it always healed itself, connecting stronger more than ever" – SELF HEALING SOUL THREAD

~ Madhurima

FOGG
FADING

TRUST THE UNIVERSE

Here Fog stands as our illusion which was there before we were born. Fog Fading is stepping out from the illusion. When we do everything right which is essential to our soul and journey path based on our intuition, without looking at the surroundings and not being disturbed by the 3d. Then every particle or you can say every scene of our story will automatically fall into their right places. This is what happening with Chanda & Madhu. Fog fading is simply clarity in vision.

It's a faith in ourselves, intuition whatever your inner selves are saying, you're trusting blindly. Even if your thought process or your decision or ideas are different from hundreds of people, you're not afraid of doing what your Intuition is saying. Just all you need to know is that your subconscious mind will suggest you "the best easiest ways" to reach your desire. You just have to trust yourself or your subconscious mind. Do remember, every path is discovered by someone and you don't need to perforce yourself to follow those steps.

Always ask a question, who said to do it that way ?? , who said there is no other way than that ?

Maybe there is a way and yet to be discovered, always choose your comfort. Like Madhu & Chanda did, both of them have been listening that "you need to do 5-6 year practice under senior editor to become executive Editor" , "you can't get to play the lead character at first , you need contacts in industry".

We never agreed what people says to us because we know we have fucking talent , Madhu can lead editors in project and Chanda can play any kind of character.

Those beliefs and declarations, It is fog fading. We all have heard this quote of Confucius *"We have two live , the second begins when we realise we only have one"*

We realised it at the perfect time and our second life begins in the second world, where the 4D world is actual and this 3D is the dead one.

In a nutshell we want that your life should be governed by you, in respect of our every relationship. At the end of the day you should be the one who's making the decision of your life.

We're not here to criticize anyone, it's just what society says ,what people say about us is their perception , we should make our own perception and philosophy.

We know the eternal fact which is our truth, your truth of life could be different from us and you will get to know when fog will fade.

We became totally new persons, who have different perceptions from others, who are more aligned with higher selves not to society.

The materialistic world is full of *MAAYA* and our human body is tasked to get ourselves detached from the *MAAYA*. All the negative one and obsession over anything is *MAAYA*, When we know the eternal truth , this materialistic world becomes a Holographic World.

In this journey of Fog fading and making our story like a Fairy tale, Bhagavad Geeta helped Chanda and Quantam Physics helped Madhu. We both are made up of Science and Spirituality. That is why we complete each other as a Soul Sister and also we want to clear one thing here...

"Science is Spirituality and Spirituality is Science" ~ Chanda

Both are two sides of one coin. Never differentiate between them and also never mix Religion with Spirituality. Religion is man-made but Spirituality is the Eternal truth of life.

SOUL

TRIBE

&

LOVE

"SOUL" is the key element of this book. Soul sister, soul searching and now soul tribe. But what is "SOUL" ? A bunch of energy working together to make an existing being in this material world and connected with one's higher self that is already in the best place in the quantum world. Yeah that's how we know the soul, a neutral energy being. So what is this soul tribe? There's a trendy internet topic that says "meet yourself, find your soul". Technically you don't have to find your soul because your existence is made of it. You actually have to meet yourself and realise your soul's existence within you. That's how it works. There's a simple way to do it, that Madhu and Chanda explored themselves. It's nothing but LOVE, self love. When you truly, wholeheartedly love yourself, prioritise yourself and gain knowledge about life and universal laws then you know how to play this game, game of life. And your soul is the connection between the 'character body' you're playing with and you (your real existence beyond the multiverse in some super world) who's controlling the remote.

So what happened when you started loving yourself, and realised your vast existence. You actually started to feel that no one but you is ruling and shaping your own life, that is you're living right now. Your whole life is a manifestation. Whoever once realised that they're on the pedestal, they stopped victimizing themselves and started to take responsibility for their lives with confidence.

Once you do that, there's no looking back, and you keep going to your best version of life. You might be thinking that what's the connection between all these and the soul tribe, right ?

When you start to see life as a game and you're a player, the body is a game slot that is given to your energy or soul to play this game. That means the place and people (basically family, it doesn't have to be because sometimes souls incarnated in their own soul tribe, but most of the time it's not the case, and one obviously can feel the difference) they don't feel like home, one never could find peace between them. I really don't have any idea how this universe always gets our back but it does. Somehow someway when your self love cup is full and you're playing your game well, you'll find them, even without trying. They just became part of your game journey, like they're destined to be together. It is said that twinflame reunion is the highest purpose of this game of life, because that makes our higher self a complete being.

Our higher self has two selves, masculine self and feminine self. And they were together, but had to be separated when incarnated, as two different human beings one who has more masculine energy is the male and one who possesses more feminine energy is the female, because it is the rule of this game, both energies just can't be incarnated together.

The same happened with Madhu and Chanda. They found soulmates in each other, that turns out as soul sisters or we can say the beginning of a soul family. And they knew like very well,the people they were living with aren't the soul family or tribe. But when these two late-teenagers remembered and felt the peace and comfort with each other, the soulmate bond unfolded. They're the best thing ever happened to them.

When the awakening phase was just gearing up, Madhu realised that 'the one' she loves, is the one, her twinflame, her multiversal eternal love.

 It's not just made up by mind it felt like an auto download from the universe to her soul. She felt something in dreams, she never had felt before. A connection, it's surreal, it's divine, something beyond this human world. And that's why she knows it is. She found her twin soul in her 18th year of life. She was so sure about him. When everyone said it's impossible, she knows it is the only thing that's possible, that's gonna work out. It's meant to be, it's destined to be. And she started walking in this game journey with it to him, to the twinflame reunion. Actually twinflames are really like this, it just takes a few moments to remember that yeah he is/she is.

{He's a celebrity to the world. A STAR people loved to gaze from distance, they don't dare to know him deeply, dive into his soul and read him, love him divinely and accept him as their very own person. But Madhu did. For her, he's the eternal homie, her human home, her twinflame, her own person}

You all might think, how I knew that HE IS.......

You all have heard about human homes, right !? But not only for saying He actually feels like my human home, the comfort the freedom I have with him is something unmatchable. I never had that. He set me free, I'm actually free with him. He lets me do, wear, eat whatever I want, go wherever I want, whenever I want. He let me be myself, and he loved me for the one I actually am. If you wanna say he has spoilt me, so yes I'm gonna accept it proudly.

That doesn't mean that he doesn't give a fuck about what I'm doing. He's so so so protective but in a good way, he let my wings flapper to fly.

He protects me from unnecessary drama, negativity, any kind of discomfort, from the hard words of society, judgements, narrow minded people and so many things.

So Madhu already has her twinflame to be reunited with and has met her soulmate, her soul sister. But what about Chanda? She finally met the love of her life. She hasn't labeled him as her twin soul or soulmate, because he's her other half. The way they both understand each other is the cherry on top of their bond. Whatever she dreamt about her partner became the reality for Chanda. It just snapped and they got connected. Whether it is Soulmate Connection or twinflame Connection every journey have a rollercoaster ride of emotions. But as love is the highest vibration that governs the universe, so when we become love everything starts to fall into the right places. Actually both Madhu's and Chanda's love was written in the stars.

Now this completed their soul tribe. And you know what Madhu's twinsoul and Chanda's highest soulmate both knew each other already and shared a really good bond. What could be best than this. Now they have their soul family completed.ss

It sounds like a fairy tale sometimes, doesn't it? A Disney love story, but it actually is, as they write their own stories. Their decade planning whatever plans they made, the projects, the travel, the night outs, the long drives, the celebrations, the work, the success and reaching heights and so on, is now made together.

GODDESS RISING & POWERS

I AM DIVINE FEMININE ENERGY. I LEAD WITH POWER AND GRACE.

In an Indian family every girl & women have listened to this compliment once in a lifetime at least *"Humari beti ghar ki Lakshmi hai."* Let me tell you guys YOU ARE in actually. Did you know what Lakshmi word means ??

It means "Lakshmi is the divine power that transforms dreams into reality".

Madhu and Chanda both are masters in this game. If anyone has any issues with law , like still you aren't able to believe in this then simply start focusing on surrounding and nature. Everyone is basically shouting about the Divine Power. Frequently you had listened to these quotes like "there is no power compared to will power, everything is inside of us and *mann ki shakti*"

When you realise all of these actually, you will feel that our ancestors are saying much more than before the modern era and THE SECRET. We realised every perception very quickly and it was totally on us what we have to adopt and we adopted what was good for our soul. In this journey the first step was "Self love". We already told you about self love in the previous chapter and that realisation of Self worth makes us QUEEN of our reality. A special mention to a queen who made us realise our power and we are queens too, is Neyah. She's a manifestation coach on YouTube. But she is much more than that to us. She's the last one we ever need to get into this vast multiversal knowledge, we are beyond grateful to her . She had taught us everything, that was overlooked by us and we needed to know in order to get whatever the fuck we want. She's a real goddess who helped us to raise the goddess in us too.

and everyone around us suddenly found us attractive , full of love and peace and we are. We didn't change our outer appearance much but still who didn't know about The laws of universe & manifestation community but their soul knows everything and they can sense divinity that awakened in us.

THE REALITY & PEDESTAL.

What's in my mind is my reality and I'm the queen of my reality , the one who's sitting on a pedestal is ME , over all the energies and emotions. It's hard to control every emotion and we should not do it actually because as a human being the minimal thing we can do is FEEL. Just feel and realise whatever life is teaching but with the attitude of Queen. So that you'll never be run by others, just only by you and you. To every men/boys, who are reading our Soul Sister right now, first of all How's you??

I hope you find this book helpful. And we just want to tell you You're KING of your reality. If you're a fully abundant mindset and you know how to transfer your dreams into reality then it means you're "The *Lakshmi*".

When we're on the path of oneness there's no gender. A girl can be Krishna and a boy can be Lakshmi. Because in the realm there's nothing on biasness, everyone's FREE.

We're glad that our Soul Partner understands this and supports it as well. Chanda & Madhu penetrated every realisation , knowledge in their subconscious and that helped them to meet "LADY BOSS" within them.

EVERGREEN

We planned the decade. Command.

Universe blessed. The rest follows.

~Madhurima

We've come to an end besties, end of this pages. But you know it's an end only to this one that describes a phase of Chanda and Madhu's life. This phase had been a game changer for both of the "SOUL SISTERS."

There's a saying "At the end everything will be fine and if not that means it's not the end". And we're ending this book with not only FINE, but with a Disney fairytale of Chanda and Madhu. Let's just take you through an imagination. Just imagine.

Madhu is waking up with her love, his hands are wrapped around her, the safest place where they feel the eternal love and peace. Her written scripts become back to back blockbusters onscreen, stealing all the best awards and internationally popular. She becomes the wonderful famous filmmaker. Her books are international bestsellers. Chanda is spending a romantic evening with her love, resting her head on his chest, living the peace of love. Her performances are appreciated by everyone, awarded by all the respected and popular award shows, her recognition and demand is on another heights in the acting industry. She becomes the amazing actress. Her books become bestsellers. Madhu and Chanda are running their own brand and production named "WE4". They have financial freedom to do everything they want. There are multiple sources of income they have, they are business owners now. Their brand is also reaching the heights. There's an overflow of money in their bank accounts. Their every project has become immensely successful, everyone knows them, loves them in the industry. They're invited to Ted talks, as best life coaches in their 20s. They started to travel the world together with their loves. Their own SUNSHINE GARDEN is growing. They're getting everything they want with just a command, like the Queens, as this reality is on their commands. They're living their best life as a fairytale, as they planned their decade and so on.

And all of you should know that all the things you've just read, is happened and happening. They made all of it a fact with their power of manifestation that y'all have too. They claimed and Universe served. That's it, that's the law. And we want you guys to also have everything you want. That's why it's a simple advice or precisely you can say a request that please just start and your life can also be a fairytale.

Now you know why the chapter name says "EVERGREEN", because the ending should be the best. And evergreen, Being Evergreen means that you are always growing into the best version of yourself. The peace and epic life they have created, something that is timeless, beyond this mundane existence, that stays a forever EVERGREEN existence of proof that Universal laws gives you power to have limitless things.

Manifestation Guide

There are so many ways that everyone is following in order to manifest their desires.

It differs from person to person. And you can easily find yours, that works best for you. Initially you have to try a few or you could possibly have your own way to manifest, that's completely new. It all works, each and every way works. Because the core is the same, you have to imprint your subconscious mind/ embody the version of yours that already living your desired reality. That's it, the rest will be done by your subconscious. It knows how to shift you according to you observed reality, dominant/ repeated thoughts or consciousness.

We're sharing that we use personally.

• We command to our subconscious mind. We command it with authority, that "my desire is mine, periodt." We command with a lil scene of visualisation (end result of our desire)

• We use subliminal. This works miracle for us, as those hidden affirmations went straight to pur subconscious mind.

That's what we do most of the time.

And there are a few more ways like Affirming, Scripting, SATs, Mind Movies, Affirmation tapes and every coach on YouTube and Instagram out there has some of their own unique ways. So basically there are so many, you choose what you wanna do. But the bottom line is "all of it works".

Procrastination

We know procrastination's habit is one of the main foe in the path of every success. It was our actually!!

So how to deal with procrastination because even though we know that we're being lazy still we does not cure because we are lazy. So in this journey to kill habit of Procrastination we learnt.

END WHAT YOU HAVE STARTED

Just complete your work without leaving it in midway. That's it !!

The ALGORITHM Metaphor

This is a metaphor, or we can say an understanding that we've got. As we know the algorithm of social media (Instagram, youtube etc.), it works like a programming that shows similar content to an user, which he/she likes to watch. Same happens with the energy vibrational algorithm. We all and everything around us are made of energy. So when our thoughts are aligned with what we desire, the algorithm starts its work. And our subconscious always takes the lead. As per the algorithm , the 3d reality moulds to show us the things that shares the same vibrational frequency (energy) with our desires/ dominant thoughts.

Our recommendations to you ~

We would like to recommend some books to reprogram your subconscious mind from authentic source.

If you still do not believe in LAWS then probably you believe in prayers, you can read

• The Power Of Subconscious Mind of Joseph Murphy

one of the easiest to understand the basics.

• Power Of Now : A Guide to Spiritual Enlightenment by Eckhart Tolle

If you used to worry about everything then you should try

• The Subtle Art of Not Giving a Fuck by Mark Manson

• Everything is Fucked by Mark Manson

To know more about Universe or Subconscious mind

• Ask and It Is Given by Esther Hicks and Jerry Hicks

• At your command, Out of this world , The Law and The Promise by Naville Goddard ,

(Basically you can buy whole collection of Naville Goddard which is easily available on online)

• Whole collection of Florence Scovel Shinn

• The Alchemist by Paulo Coelho

For better Financial knowledge or how to maintain Abundance

•Rich dad poor dad by Robert Kiyosaki and Sharon Lechter

• Think & Grow Rich by Napoleon Hill

• Psychology of Money by Morgan Housel

For Advance understanding of Universal Laws

• Becoming Supernatural. How Common People Are Doing The Uncommon, Book by Joe Dispenza

• Reality Transurfing. Steps I-V , Book by Vadim Zeland

You can find us on Instagram, besties ☺

@chandajaiswaro8 (Chanda)

@darker_shade_of_brightness (Madhurima)

{ALL DOODLES, USED IN THIS BOOK, ARE TAKEN FROM PINTEREST. ALL THE RIGHTS AND CREDITS GO TO THE RESPECTIVE ARTISTS. THANK YOU SO MUCH FOR THOSE AMAZING ARTWORKS, THAT MAKES OUR BOOK WAY MORE AESTHETIC}

Acknowledgement

The four phases we have mentioned in "Soul Sisters" . It comes in every single person's life , there is no written that Not awakening phase is only happens in teenage of life , People DISORIENTED in 20's , Awakening comes in 30's and people enlightened in 50's or 60's age of life. Some people are disoriented in 40's too and some people who are just in his/her 20's or 30's are living in enlightenment phase.

Happiness, Grief, Love , Hate it's all is just a state of mind , our Subconscious is the only door and reason for whatever happening and going to happen with ourselves. People can do time travel and elapse this phases in their 20's too.

Like we did, we're in our Enlightenment phase but it doesn't mean we never felt something negative or not be triggered of any situation.

It's just our way of handling situation is changed!

That's what we tried to make people understand about themselves through our story.

Through those phases you could learn and analysis your current phase, where you're right now.